THE TEN COMMANDMENTS

...elp
junior highers apply
God's laws to their lives

by Paul Woods

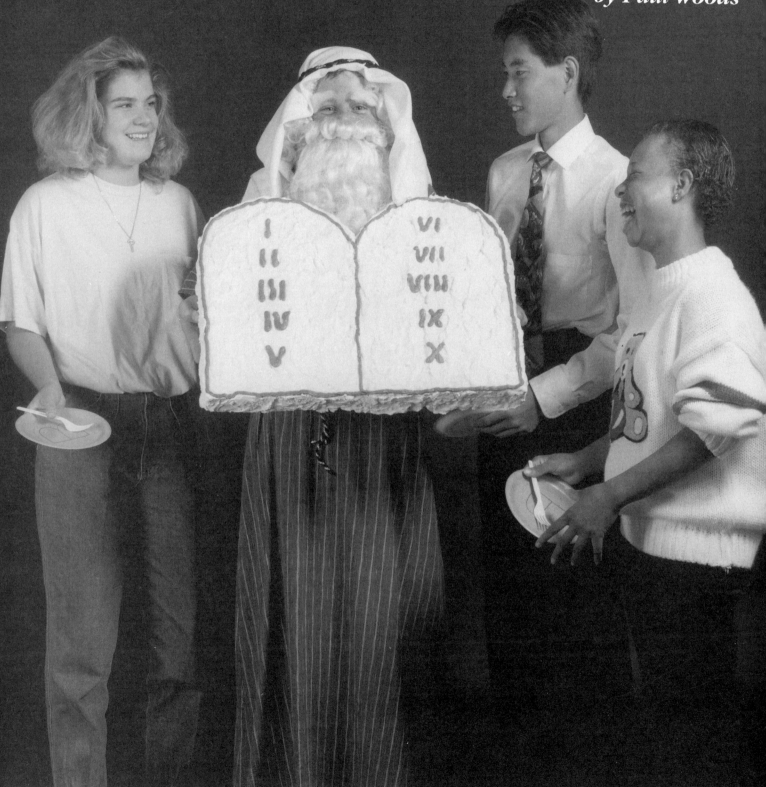

Group
Loveland, Colorado

Credits
Edited by Michael Warden
Cover designed by Jill Nordbye and DeWain Stoll
Cover photo by Jeff Buehler
Interior designed by Judy Bienick and Jan Aufdemberge
Illustrations by Raymond Medici

ISBN 1-55945-127-0
Printed in the United States of America.

CONTENTS

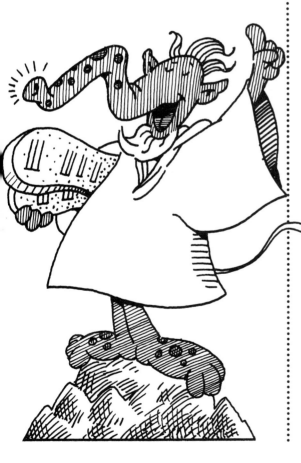

THE TEN COMMANDMENTS

To say that teenagers today are known for breaking the law is probably an understatement. Since 1950, juvenile delinquency has increased by 250 percent in the United States. Twenty-two percent of high school seniors say they've gotten into trouble with the police at least once in the past year. Thirty-two percent admit to having stolen something at least once. And a look at the box below tells us many teenagers are into serious crime as well.

The Ten Commandments are the center of God's law as given to the Old Testament Israelites. They express the heart of how God wants us to live. Most of the laws teenagers break today are based on these old laws given by God.

Type of Crime	Arson	Burglaries	Motor Vehicle Theft	Larceny-theft
Percent Committed by Kids Under 18	41.2%	38.0%	38.0%	32.8%

Contrary to popular opinion, God's laws aren't just a bunch of arbitrary rules designed to make life miserable for us. God gave us laws for much the same reason that a mother tells her child not to play in the street. God loves us, and gave us the Ten Commandments to guide us toward living a safe and fulfilling life.

Standing alone, each of the Ten Commandments makes sense, even in today's fast-paced world. But in the New Testament, we find Jesus adding new dimensions to the commandments, taking them a step beyond simple obedience. Jesus points out that the attitudes behind obedience are just as important as the obedience itself. He says we can break the commandments in our hearts without breaking them with our actions at all.

That sounds like bad news. After all, who among us can keep his or her thoughts in check 100 percent of the time? But the bad news becomes good news when we look at the Ten Commandments through the filter of Christ's death and resurrection. Through Jesus' work on the cross, he pulled the curtains on the punishing effects of the Law, and ushered in the time of mercy and grace, which we still live in today.

Even though we break God's laws—by action or by thought—we can receive forgiveness through the sacrifice of Jesus Christ. God's laws now show us more clearly our need for him.

Different denominations separate the Ten Commandments in different ways. So to avoid any such problems, the commandments are referred to by their verse numbers in Exodus 20. Whatever your system for numbering the commandments, you'll be able to use this course without any problems.

As you use this course, you'll help your junior highers and middle schoolers better understand God as they learn about the laws he's given us. They'll be challenged not just to obey the laws, but to practice the attitudes Jesus says will lead to obeying the laws naturally. And kids will be encouraged to show their love for God as they discover his heart of love for them.

By the end of this course your students will:
● understand God's reasons for giving the Ten Commandments;
● learn more about what it means to really love God;
● see the importance of respecting and honoring others; and
● begin to treat others the way they themselves want to be treated.

COURSE OBJECTIVES

HOW TO USE THIS COURSE

ACTIVE LEARNING

Think back on an important lesson you've learned in life. Did you learn it from reading about it? from hearing about it? from something you experienced? Chances are, the most important lessons you've learned came from something you've experienced. That's what active learning is—learning by doing. And active learning is a key element in Group's Active Bible Curriculum.

Active learning leads students in doing things that help them understand important principles, messages and ideas. It's a discovery process that helps kids internalize what they learn.

Each lesson section in Group's Active Bible Curriculum plays an important part in active learning:

The **Opener** involves kids in the topic in fun and unusual ways.

The **Action and Reflection** includes an experience designed to evoke specific feelings in the students. This section also processes those feelings through "How did you feel?" questions and applies the message to situations kids face.

The **Bible Application** actively connects the topic with the Bible. It helps kids see how the Bible is relevant to the situations they face.

The **Commitment** helps students internalize the Bible's message and commit to make changes in their lives.

The **Closing** funnels the lesson's message into a time of creative reflection and prayer.

When you put all the sections together, you get a lesson that's fun to teach. And kids get messages they'll remember.

BEFORE THE 4-WEEK SESSION

● Read the Introduction, the Course Objectives and This Course at a Glance.

● Decide how you'll publicize the course using the clip art on the Publicity Page (p. 9). Prepare fliers, newsletter articles and posters as needed.

● Look at the Bonus Ideas (p. 41) and decide which ones you'll use.

● Read the opening statements, Objectives and Bible Basis for the lesson. The Bible Basis shows how specific passages relate to junior highers and middle schoolers today.

● Choose which Opener and Closing options to use. Each is appropriate for a different kind of group.

● Gather necessary supplies from This Lesson at a Glance.

● Read each section of the lesson. Adjust where necessary for your class size and meeting room.

● The approximate minutes listed give you an idea of how long each activity will take. Each lesson is designed to take 35 to 60 minutes. Shorten or lengthen activities as needed to fit your group.

● If you see you're going to have extra time, do an activity or two from the "If You Still Have Time . . . " box or from the Bonus Ideas (p. 41).

● Dive into the activities with the kids. Don't be a spectator. The lesson will be more successful and rewarding to both you and your students.

● Though some kids may at first think certain activities are "silly," they'll enjoy them and they'll remember the messages from these activities long after the lesson is over. As one Active Bible Curriculum user has said, "I can ask the kids questions about a lesson I did three weeks ago and they actually remember what I taught!" And that's the whole idea of teaching . . . isn't it?

Have fun with the activities you lead. Remember, it is Jesus who encourages us to become "as little children." Besides, how often do your kids get *permission* to express their childlike qualities?

HELPFUL HINTS

● The answers given after discussion questions are responses your students *might* give. They aren't the only answers or the "right" answers. If needed, use them to spark discussion. Kids won't always say what you wish they'd say. That's why some of the responses given are negative or controversial. If someone responds negatively, don't be shocked. Accept the person and use the opportunity to explore other angles of the issue.

THIS COURSE AT A GLANCE

Before you dive into the lessons, familiarize yourself with each lesson aim. Then read the scripture passages.
- Study them as a background to the lessons.
- Use them as a basis for your personal devotions.
- Think about how they relate to kids' circumstances today.

LESSON 1: TEN TO LIVE BY

Lesson Aim: To help junior highers understand God's reasons for giving the Ten Commandments.

Bible Basis: Exodus 20:1-17; Matthew 5:17-19 and Romans 13:8-10.

LESSON 2: HEART, SOUL AND MIND

Lesson Aim: To help junior highers understand what it means to love God.

Bible Basis: Exodus 20:2-11 and Matthew 22:36-38.

LESSON 3: OTHERS BEFORE SELF

Lesson Aim: To help junior highers learn to honor and respect others.

Bible Basis: Exodus 20:12-14; Matthew 5:21-22, 27-28 and Mark 7:8-13.

LESSON 4: DON'T BE GREEDY

Lesson Aim: To help junior highers learn to trust God for things they need, and to treat others the way they want to be treated.

Bible Basis: Exodus 20:15-17; Matthew 6:25-34 and Matthew 7:12.

PUBLICITY PAGE

Grab your junior highers' attention! Photocopy this page, and then cut out and paste the clip art of your choice in your church bulletin or newsletter to advertise this course on the Ten Commandments. Or photocopy and use the ready-made flier as a bulletin insert. Permission to photocopy this clip art is granted for local church use.

Splash the clip art on posters, fliers or even postcards! Just add the vital details: the date and time the course begins and where you'll meet.

It's that simple.

THE TEN COMMANDMENTS

A 4-week junior high and middle school course on understanding the 10 most important laws God ever gave

Come to _____

On _____

At _____

Come learn how to make the Ten Commandments come alive in your daily life!

TEN TO LIVE BY

To most junior highers and middle schoolers, the Ten Commandments are a mysterious bunch of regulations given to another nation centuries ago. Kids don't understand why God gave the Law or how it relates to their lives today. Help kids see that God's giving of the Ten Commandments was a loving act designed to help his people—both then and now.

To help junior highers understand God's reasons for giving the Ten Commandments.

LESSON AIM

Students will:
- **discuss how we tell the difference between good and bad;**
- **experience what it's like to play a game without rules;**
- **explore how the Ten Commandments apply to life today; and**
- **commit to follow God by obeying his commandments as fully as possible.**

OBJECTIVES

Look up the following scriptures. Then read the background paragraphs to see how the passages relate to your junior highers and middle schoolers.

In **Exodus 20:1-17**, Moses reports to the people of Israel the laws God gave him on stone tablets.

Commonly known as the Ten Commandments, these laws formed the basis of what the Jews knew simply as The Law. God wanted his people to obey these commandments, but not just to make him happy. He knew that living by the Ten Commandments pointed the way to a higher plane of living we now know as Christianity.

Today's teenagers need to realize why God gave the law—not to put impossible restrictions on people, but to draw them to faith in him and to help them live their lives in harmony with one another.

BIBLE BASIS
EXODUS 20:1-17
MATTHEW 5:17-19
ROMANS 13:8-10

Jesus speaks in **Matthew 5:17-19** of the enduring importance of the law.

Jesus wanted his hearers to know that the things he was teaching were not really changing what the people had been taught for hundreds of years. Rather, Jesus' teachings were explanations of what it *really* meant to live by the law.

Kids tend to think of the Old Testament as ancient history—no longer valid. But the principles behind the Ten Commandments are the same principles Jesus taught, and still apply to our lives today.

In **Romans 13:8-10**, Paul points out that the law is about loving God and loving other people.

Paul calls love the fulfillment of the law, because if we really do love God and other people the way God wants us to, we'll naturally obey the commands the law gives.

Kids need to see that obeying the Ten Commandments isn't just sticking to a set of rules. It's an attitude—a way of life—that constantly seeks to love God more and to share that love with other people.

THIS LESSON AT A GLANCE

Section	Minutes	What Students Will Do	Supplies
Opener (Option 1)	5 to 10	**Bad News**—Search old newspapers and magazines for bad things people have done.	Newspapers, magazines
(Option 2)		**Against the Law?**—Brainstorm laws and discuss their value.	Chalkboard and chalk or newsprint and markers
Action and Reflection	10 to 15	**Wrecked Race**—Participate in a race where they really don't know what to do to win.	Masking tape, balloons, pails, spoons
Bible Application	10 to 15	**Alien Invasion**—Pretend to be aliens figuring out what the Ten Commandments are all about.	Bibles
Commitment	10 to 15	**Zoobladite Law**—Compare fictional laws with God's commandments.	Bibles, "Zoobladite Ten Commandments" handouts (p. 17)
Closing (Option 1)	up to 5	**Election Day**—Vote on which set of laws they'd rather live by.	Bibles, "Zoobladite Ten Commandments" handouts (p. 17)
(Option 2)		**A Piece of the Rock**—Receive small stones to remind them of the laws God gave us.	Bibles, small stones

The Lesson

☐ OPTION 1: BAD NEWS

Form groups of two or three and pass out old newspapers and magazines. Tell groups to find people who've done bad things and tear out the page or article. Have kids discuss each situation in their groups to be sure they agree that the person has done something bad. After about three minutes, call kids back together and have groups briefly report what they found.

After each group reports, ask the rest of the kids if they agree with the group's choices. If kids disagree, have them explain why.

When all the groups have reported, ask:

● **How did you decide which people had done bad things?** (They hurt other people; they broke laws.)

● **Was there any disagreement in your group about someone you wanted to choose? Why or why not?** (Yes, we had different opinions about what was bad; no, we all agreed they'd broken laws.)

● **Would your task have been harder if our society had no rules or laws to live by?** (Yes, it would have been tough to say who was bad; no, we would have sensed who was bad anyway.)

Say: **Today we're beginning a study of the Ten Commandments, the most important laws God gave to the people of Israel. We're going to look first at why God gave those commandments and what they mean for us.**

☐ OPTION 2: AGAINST THE LAW?

Begin by having kids brainstorm rules or laws they know of. Write an abbreviated form of each one on a chalkboard or newsprint. After you have a list of 15 or more, stop the brainstorming and ask:

● **Which of these laws do you feel are good? Explain.**

● **Which do you think are bad? Explain.**

● **What makes a law good?** (A law is good if it helps people; it's good if it keeps people out of danger.)

Say: **Today we're beginning a study of the Ten Commandments, the most important laws God gave to the people of Israel. We're going to look first at why God gave those commandments and what they mean for us.**

WRECKED RACE

Form two teams. Have teams gather at one end of the room and place a piece of masking tape across the other end of the room. Give each team three balloons, a pail and two spoons.

Say: **The object of this game is to be the first team finished. Go!**

When kids start asking what they're supposed to do, say: **You're supposed to finish first. The rest you have to figure out for yourselves.**

Let kids try to play the game. If any team does what's described below, stop the game and declare that team the winner. If not, keep teams trying until you stop the game after about five minutes.

Say: **What I wanted you to do was to have two people use the spoons to carry a balloon down to the tape and back without touching the balloon with their hands, then deposit the balloon in the pail and give the spoons to the next pair, who would take the next balloon. The first team with all three balloons in or on the pail would have won.**

Ask:

● **How did you feel trying to play this game?** (Silly, we didn't know what to do; it wasn't really a game without rules.)

● **What made this game difficult?** (No instructions were given; we didn't have any rules.)

● **How would this be like trying to please God without knowing what he wanted us to do?** (It would be tough to know what pleased him; people would just be doing whatever they wanted.)

ALIEN INVASION

Say: **Imagine you're all Zoobladites from the planet Zoobladoo. You've just secretly landed on this planet and assumed the identities of earthlings, but you don't know how earthlings are supposed to act. You want to figure out how to act to keep your identity secret. You sneak into a big empty building and find a huge book lying open on a table. The first thing you read is Exodus 20:1-17.**

Read the passage aloud, then say: **After reading that, you figure it must be the most important laws of earthlings. But with your super-reading speed, you zoom through the rest of the book to find out more about these laws and what they mean in Earth society.**

Form groups of four or five Zoobladites and assign Matthew 5:17-19 or Romans 13:8-10 to each group. Have groups each study their passage and refer back to Exodus 20:1-17 to determine how the laws God gave Moses are to be used today. Remind kids that they're Zoobladites, not earthlings, and they're trying to learn how to be good earthlings so that they won't be easily detected as aliens.

After groups have completed their research, have them report on what the Ten Commandments mean for today.

Ask:

● **Are these laws still important today? Explain.** (Yes, Jesus said they were; no, loving people is more important.)

● **What does love have to do with the Ten Commandments?** (Nothing, they're just laws; the laws help us understand loving God and other people.)

● **Why did God give us the Ten Commandments?** (To help us learn to love him and each other; because he loves us and he knew we needed guidelines to live by.)

Say: **Looking at the Ten Commandments from the perspective of aliens can bring new understanding to these important rules for living. But what are we to do with these commandments? Let's compare God's commandments to the fictional Zoobladite commandments to help us discover how we should respond.**

ZOOBLADITE LAW

Give kids each a Bible. Then pass out copies of the "Zoobladite Ten Commandments" handout (p. 17) and explain that these are the 10 most important Zoobladite laws. Have kids form pairs and examine the handouts, and compare the Zoobladite laws with the Ten Commandments in Exodus 2:1-17. Have kids determine which of the Zoobladite laws are good and which are bad. After about five minutes, have pairs discuss what they decided. Then ask:

● **How are God's laws different from the Zoobladite laws?** (God's laws are for our own good; Zoobladite laws seem to be for someone else's good.)

● **What's an appropriate response to the God who gave us the Ten Commandments?** (Obey him; love him back.)

Have kids return to their pairs and tell each other one good thing they see in their partner's obedience to God's commands. For example, someone might say, "You always show respect to your parents," or "You never complain about wanting things other people have." Then have partners say a brief prayer together, committing to respond to God's love by serving and obeying him as fully as possible.

C O M M I T M E N T
(10 to 15 minutes)

Table Talk

The Table Talk activity in this course helps junior highers and middle schoolers discuss with their parents the Ten Commandments.

If you choose to use the Table Talk activity, this is a good time to show students the "Table Talk" handout (p. 18). Ask them to spend time with their parents completing it.

Before kids leave, give them each the "Table Talk" handout to take home, or tell them you'll be sending it to their parents. Tell kids to each be prepared to report on their experience based on the handout next week.

Or use the Table Talk idea found in the Bonus Ideas (p. 42) for a meeting based on the handout.

CLOSING
(up to 5 minutes)

☐ OPTION 1: ELECTION DAY

Have kids look at Exodus 20:1-17 again and at the "Zoobladite Ten Commandments." Then have students vote on which set of rules they'd rather live by. Have kids each explain why they voted the way they did.

Say: **Unlike the Zoobladite's religion, our God's laws demonstrate his immense love for each of us.**

Close with prayer, thanking God for giving us guidelines to live by that are meant to help us as well as honor him.

☐ OPTION 2: A PIECE OF THE ROCK

Read aloud Exodus 20:1-17 again. Say: **The Ten Commandments were written by God himself on tablets of stone. I'm going to give each of you a small stone to keep as a reminder of the tablets of stone the Ten Commandments were written on.**

Before you close with prayer, encourage kids to each think of God's love and their commitment to respond in love.

If You Still Have Time . . .

Today's Commandments?—Form groups of no more than five. Have groups each brainstorm a list of the rules they deal with every day at school and home. Have kids discuss how rules differ from the Ten Commandments.

Commandment Rap—Have kids write a rap listing the Ten Commandments and describing how they apply today. Then have kids perform the rap for another Sunday school class or during your church service.

Zoobladite
Ten Commandments

Examine these laws and determine which are good and which are bad.

1. You will obey the Supreme Zoobladite, no matter what he says.

2. You will give the Supreme Zoobladite one-half of everything you earn.

3. You will immediately kill anyone you hear speaking against the Supreme Zoobladite.

4. You will not kill anyone for any other reason.

5. You will not take anything from anyone poorer than you.

6. You can take whatever you want from Zoobladites richer than you, as long as you don't get caught in the act.

7. You will treat your children as slaves until the first time they beat you up.

8. You will obey your parents until you think you can whip them in a fight.

9. Any female Zoobladite can marry up to five male Zoobladites, but no male Zoobladite can marry more than one female Zoobladite.

10. You will work for 100 zeens and then get 10 zeens off to do whatever you want.

Table Talk

To the Parent: We're involved in a junior high course at church called *The Ten Commandments*. Students are exploring why God gave us the Ten Commandments and how they apply to us today. We'd like you and your teenager to spend some time discussing this important topic. Use this "Table Talk" page to help you do that.

Parent

Complete the following sentences:
● When I was a junior higher, I thought the Ten Commandments were . . .
● The rules I liked least while growing up were . . .
● One thing I always had a tough time understanding about the Ten Commandments was . . .

Junior higher

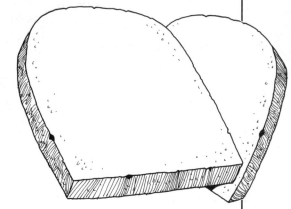

Complete the following sentences:
● I always thought the Ten Commandments were . . .
● The rules I like following the least are . . .
● I know rules are valuable because . . .

Parent and Junior higher

Take turns answering the following questions:
● What's the value of the Ten Commandments today?
● Is it important to follow the Ten Commandments today?
● What did Jesus' ministry tell us about the Ten Commandments?
● Why was it difficult for people to completely follow the Ten Commandments?
● Which commandments are easiest to follow? toughest? Explain.

Read together Exodus 20:1-17; Matthew 22:34-40; and 2 Corinthians 5:14-21. Discuss these passages and how Jesus redefined the commandments through his ministry, death and resurrection.

HEART, SOUL AND MIND

Love is a tainted word in our society. But God knows what true love is—he demonstrated it for us. And he wants us to truly love him.

The first 11 verses of Exodus 20 give us guidance on how to really love God. Help your kids understand, in a practical way, what that means in a Christian teenager's life.

To help junior highers understand what it means to love God.

LESSON AIM

Students will:
- think about how people have shown love to their gods;
- write a letter to someone they really care about;
- determine how to explain Exodus 20:2-11 to a first-grader; and
- commit to love God more in a specific way.

OBJECTIVES

Look up the following scriptures. Then read the background paragraphs to see how the passages relate to your junior highers and middle schoolers.

In **Exodus 20:2-11,** God gives the Israelites the beginning of his 10 most important guidelines for living.

These first verses in Exodus 20 relate almost exclusively to the individual's relationship with God. God lets his people know that he is not to be considered just one more god to worship along with other gods, but that he is the only true God and that they are to worship him alone.

Our God is a loving God. But he's also a God of awesome power. Kids need to realize that the God they love must be

BIBLE BASIS

EXODUS 20:2-11
MATTHEW 22:36-38

treated with the love and reverence he deserves as the creator of our universe.

In **Matthew 22:36-38**, Jesus tells a critic what is the most important of the commandments.

Jesus' response to the Pharisee affirmed and summarized the commandments related to our relationship with God. Notice that he responded not by reciting the letter of the law, but by giving the attitude of the heart that would result in one's following the fine points of what the law demanded.

The same attitude Jesus pointed to is what we all need today: loving God with our whole selves. If we can help kids do that, obedience to his commands will follow.

THIS LESSON AT A GLANCE

Section	Minutes	What Students Will Do	Supplies
Opener (Option 1)	5 to 10	**How They Love Gods**—See how different people in the Bible showed love to their gods.	Gummi Bears candies or other animal candies, Bibles
(Option 2)		**Gods of Snow**—Make paper snowmen and think about how to worship an idol.	Paper, tape, markers
Action and Reflection	10 to 15	**Love Letters**—Each write a letter to the person they care about most.	Paper, pencils
Bible Application	10 to 15	**Zoobladite Tutors**—Explain Exodus 20:2-11 so that a first-grader could understand it.	"Loving God" handouts (p.25), pencils, Bible
Commitment	10 to 15	**Love, Biblical Style**—Brainstorm specific ways to love God more.	Newsprint and markers or chalkboard and chalk, tape
Closing (Option 1)	up to 5	**Bowing Down**—Kneel to offer prayers of praise and thanksgiving.	

The Lesson

OPENER
(5 to 10 minutes)

☐ OPTION 1: HOW THEY LOVE GODS

As kids arrive, give them each a candy. Don't let kids eat their bears right away. When you're ready, form three groups based on the colors of kids' bears. Say: **Today we're going to look at some commandments that help us know** how to really love God. But first, let's see how some people in the Bible worshiped their gods.

Give each group one of these passages: 2 Chronicles 33:21-22; Psalm 106:37-39; or Daniel 3:13-27. Have groups each look up their passage and report on what the people in the passage did to show they loved their god.

After groups have reported, ask:

● **How are your Gummi Bears candies like the false gods these people worshiped long ago?** (They look like little idols; our groups are divided under different-color bears, just as different people served different gods back then.)

● **Do people today do things like those described in these passages? Explain.** (Yes, in Satan worship; no, not any more.)

● **Are these the kinds of things the Bible teaches that God wants from us? Explain.** (No, he just wants us to live for him; I don't know.)

Say: **The first several verses of the Ten Commandments concentrate specifically on how we are to show God we love him. And we're going to dig into those commandments today.**

Have kids eat their bears.

☐ OPTION 2: GODS OF SNOW

Pass out paper, tape and markers. Have kids each make a "snowman" by wadding up paper and fastening the wads together. Encourage kids to add any creative touches they want to. Give them about three minutes to work.

Then ask:

● **If this snowman was a god, how would you show your love to it?** (Give it things; pray to it.)

● **How does that compare to how God might want us to show our love to him?** (He'd like the same things; he wouldn't want our trinkets.)

● **If you were God, the creator of the universe, how would you want people to show their love to you?** (Give me lots of gold; bow down and pray to me; obey me; love me.)

Say: **People show love to their gods in different ways. But our God, the true God, gave us instructions for how to show love to him in the Ten Commandments. We're going to look at those commandments today.**

Have kids each throw away their snowman to symbolize doing away with idols so they can better serve God.

Table Talk Follow-Up

If you sent the "Table Talk" handout (p. 18) to parents last week, discuss students' reactions to the activity. Ask volunteers to share what they learned from the discussion with their parents.

ACTION AND REFLECTION
(10 to 15 minutes)

BIBLE APPLICATION
(10 to 15 minutes)

LOVE LETTERS

Pass out paper and pencils. Say: **Think about the adult in your life who you care about the most. It might be your mother, father, another relative or a close friend.**

Pause to let kids choose who to think about. Then say: **Now imagine you're leaving to live with a group of other students in a major scientific research project. You won't be able to communicate with the outside world for 10 years. What would you want to say to the person who means so much to you before you leave? What would you want to make sure that person knows while you're gone for 10 years? Write your thoughts in a letter to that person, without naming the person in the letter.**

Give kids about seven minutes to write. Then have volunteers read aloud what they wrote. Ask:

● **What feelings did you have as you thought about what to write?** (Sadness; thankfulness.)

● **What inspired those feelings?** (How much I love her; everything he's done for me.)

● **How might that be like God wants us to feel toward him?** (We should love him much more; he wants us to be thankful.)

● **If we love God as much as or more than we love that one special person, how should we show that love to him?** (Obeying him; thanking him for what he's done.)

Say: **There are lots of ways to show God we love him. Let's use a part of the Ten Commandments to help us find out what some of those ways are. But first we'll re-introduce some old friends.**

ZOOBLADITE TUTORS

Say: **Remember the Zoobladites? They're still around. They've been studying the first part of the Ten Commandments and want to teach them to their children. But they need your help.**

Form groups of about six. Give groups each a "Loving God" handout (p. 25) and a pencil. Have groups each go through their handout, writing down how they'd explain each section of the commandments to a Zoobladite first-grader.

When groups have completed their handouts, let them each report what they wrote. Then ask:

● **From all you've studied, how does God want us to show him love?** (Serving him alone as God; set aside one day especially for him and for rest.)

This would be a good place to explain your church's teaching on the observance of the Sabbath and how that relates to today. You might want to ask your pastor or another church leader to come to class to discuss this issue with your kids.

Say: **Jesus also had something to say about this part of the Ten Commandments. Let's read Matthew 22:36-38.**

Have a volunteer read aloud the passage, then ask:

● **What does it really mean to "Love the Lord your God with all your heart and with all your soul and with all your mind"?** (To serve him in everything; to keep him at the center of every part of our lives.)

LOVE, BIBLICAL STYLE

Say: **Let's think a little more about what it means to really love God the way Jesus said we should.**

Tape a sheet of newsprint to the wall or use a chalkboard. Have kids brainstorm one- or two-word ideas of ways to love God the way the Bible tells us to. List the words as they're given, such as give, love others, obey.

After you have a list of at least 10 ideas, have kids stop and think about what they've listed. Encourage kids each to choose two or three ideas they want to work on in their life. Then have kids each come up to the newsprint silently and write their initials next to the ideas they've chosen as a commitment to carry out those ideas this week.

After kids have each initialed the newsprint, form pairs. Have kids each scan the newsprint, then compliment their partner on one way they see their partner already showing love for God. For example, someone might say: "Andy, I really admire the way you're always trying to help other people. It shows how much you love God."

☐ OPTION 1: BOWING DOWN

When pairs are finished, call everyone together and say: **One way people in the Old Testament showed their love and reverence for God was to bow before him. Some even threw themselves flat on their faces to show their humility. People often get down on their knees to pray, to demonstrate their reverence for God. Let's kneel today for our closing prayer and offer brief prayers of thanksgiving and praise to our God to show our love for him.**

Kneel with your kids and begin the prayer time. Close with "amen" when all the kids who wish to have prayed.

☐ OPTION 2: THANK YOU NOTES

Pass out half-sheets of paper and have kids fold them in half. On the inside, have them each write a simple note of praise and thanks to God, as if they were actually going to send it to him. Encourage kids to include in the note the specific commitment they made to love him more.

When kids are finished, have volunteers close in prayer, using thoughts from their notes. Encourage kids to each take their note home as a reminder of what God's done for them and of what they committed to do to love him more.

COMMITMENT
(10 to 15 minutes)

CLOSING
(up to 5 minutes)

If You Still Have Time . . .

Personal Pantomime—Have individuals each pantomime their response to the words of God as you read through Exodus 20:2-11 aloud. Pause after each sentence for kids to pantomime their actions.

Gods Before Him—Brainstorm a list of modern gods. Start with ones adults might be accused of worshiping, such as money and career. Then brainstorm ones junior highers might worship, such as popularity or the right sneakers.

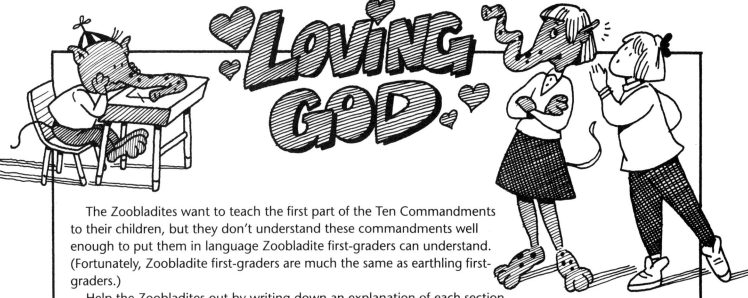

Loving God

The Zoobladites want to teach the first part of the Ten Commandments to their children, but they don't understand these commandments well enough to put them in language Zoobladite first-graders can understand. (Fortunately, Zoobladite first-graders are much the same as earthling first-graders.)

Help the Zoobladites out by writing down an explanation of each section below in language a first-grader could understand.

Exodus 20:1-11

And God spoke all these words: I am the Lord your God, who brought you out of Egypt, out of the land of slavery. You shall have no other gods before me.

You shall not make for yourself an idol in the form of anything in heaven above or on the earth beneath or in the waters below.

You shall not bow down to them or worship them; for I, the Lord your God, am a jealous God, punishing the children for the sin of the fathers to the third and fourth generation of those who hate me, but showing love to a thousand generations of those who love me and keep my commandments.

You shall not misuse the name of the Lord your God, for the Lord will not hold anyone guiltless who misuses his name.

Remember the Sabbath day by keeping it holy. Six days you shall labor and do all your work, but the seventh day is a Sabbath to the Lord your God. On it you shall not do any work, neither you, nor your son or daughter, nor your manservant or maidservant, nor your animals, nor the alien within your gates.

For in six days the Lord made the heavens and the earth, the sea, and all that is in them, but he rested on the seventh day. Therefore the Lord blessed the Sabbath day and made it holy.

LESSON 3

OTHERS BEFORE SELF

Our society says: "Look out for yourself! Defend your rights! Grab all you can get!"

But that's not God's way.

God says honor others and place their rights above your own. This message can be tough for junior highers to accept. They see their peers fighting to get all they can, and feel like they should be able to do that too. Help your kids see that following God's way is better—fighting for your own way can bring short-term results, but it can never bring long-term happiness.

LESSON AIM

To help junior highers learn to honor and respect others.

OBJECTIVES

Students will:
- play a game to help them feel what it's like to be dishonored and disrespected;
- examine what Jesus said about three of the commandments;
- write an acrostic about honor and respect; and
- pray about showing more honor and respect to parents and others.

BIBLE BASIS

EXODUS 20:12-14
MATTHEW 5:21-22, 27-28
MARK 7:8-13

Look up the following scriptures. Then read the background paragraphs to see how the passages relate to your junior highers and middle schoolers.

In **Exodus 20:12-14**, God gives commands to honor father and mother, don't murder and don't commit adultery.

In these three commandments, God sets up some basic rules for relationships with other people. The commandment about honoring parents is the first commandment to include a promise, and it gives parents their proper place of respect. The other two of these commandments tell us of the respect we should have for the sanctity of life and how we should respect other people.

These commandments can help kids today develop more respect for others as they see what God has to say about honoring others through our attitudes and actions.

In **Matthew 5:21-22, 27-28** and **Mark 7:8-13** Jesus gives us new insights into the commandments in Exodus.

Jesus sees the commandments as more than just rules to be followed. He sees them as attitudes of the mind and heart. As with the earlier commandments, Jesus indicates that what's in a person's heart is just as important as what the person does.

Kids can learn that obeying the letter of the law won't please God if they're doing it with the wrong attitude. Truly honoring and respecting others is the key to these commandments.

THIS LESSON AT A GLANCE

Section	Minutes	What Students Will Do	Supplies
Opener (Option 1)	5 to 10	**Perfect Children?**—Discuss how children on television act toward their parents.	
(Option 2)		**Great or Ghastly Greeting**—Experience being greeted in two very different ways.	
Action and Reflection	10 to 15	**Playing the Game**—Play a game in which they feel a lack of respect and honor.	Chairs, music for the game, "Capture the Chairs" handout (p. 32), scissors
Bible Application	15 to 20	**Zoobladite Zingers**—Answer questions about Jesus' comments on the commandments.	"Zoobladite Zingers" handouts (p. 33), Bibles
Commitment	5 to 10	**Respect and Honor Acrostic**—Write an acrostic symbolizing the word "respect" or "honor."	Paper, pencils
Closing (Option 1)	up to 5	**Prayer of Respect**—Tell God how they'll respect others more.	
(Option 2)		**Pairs in Prayer**—Copy their acrostic and tell a partner about it.	3×5 cards, pencils

The Lesson

☐ OPTION 1: PERFECT CHILDREN?

Have kids call out TV shows they watch that show parents and children interacting. Have them vote and choose their three favorites. Then for each of the top three have volunteers act out a sample scene of parents and kids interacting on the show.

Afterward, ask:

● **How do the kids in the show treat the parents?** (They don't respect parents; they're pretty kind to parents.)

● **Would your parents allow you to treat them the way the kids in the show treat their parents? should they?**

● **Do you think God would be pleased with the way the kids in the show treat their parents? Explain.** (No, God wants us to respect parents; yes, the kids are generally nice to their parents.)

Say: **Today we're going to be looking at three commandments that deal with respecting and honoring others. One of those commandments is about honoring our parents.**

☐ OPTION 2: GREAT OR GHASTLY GREETING

Enlist the help of two of your most outgoing students to help with this activity. Before class, tell the two they are going to be greeting everyone who comes to class. Have them arrive early, and tell one to be extremely polite and respectful. Tell the other to be just the opposite. For example, the first might tell Susan: "Hi, Susan! Sure glad to see you today! Come on in and find a good seat!" The other might say: "Oh, it's only you. I guess you can sit wherever you want, as long as it's far away from me!"

After all the kids have arrived and been greeted, ask:

● **How did it feel to be greeted as you arrived for class today?** (Great; I wondered what was going on.)

● **Did you notice any difference in the way the two greeters greeted? Explain.** (Yes, one was nice and the other was a jerk; yes, one liked me and the other didn't.)

Let kids know that the greeters were instructed to act the way they did.

Ask:

● **What made the difference in the way the two made you feel?** (I felt respected by one; one didn't seem to care if I was there or not.)

● **Are you ever treated the way the "disrespectful" greeter treated you?** (Yes, all the time; no, I'd hurt anyone who tried to treat me like that.)

● **How are the feelings you had today like the ones you**

have when you're treated badly by others? (Kids at school are a lot worse; I usually feel angry toward people who treat me badly.)

Say: **The way someone treats you can make or break your day. Today we're looking at commandments that deal with our relationships with other people and how we should treat others.**

PLAYING THE GAME

Form two equal teams. Arrange chairs in a circle for musical chairs, being sure to set out one less chair than you have people. Have someone ready to start and stop the music for the game.

Say: **Now we're going to have a little fun playing a game. It's called Capture the Chairs. Here are your instructions.**

Cut apart and pass out the appropriate part of the "Capture the Chairs" handout (p. 32) to each team. Let teams read their instructions and prepare to play the game. When you're ready to start, line the kids up so that no two team members are next to each other, if possible.

Start the music and let the action begin!

When one team has won, have kids return to their regular seating and discuss these questions:

● **What surprised you about this game?** (The other team kept fighting for the seats; the other team didn't even put up a fight.)

● **How did it feel to be the team that let others have the chairs?** (I felt fine since I knew we were winning; I kept wanting to fight for a chair too.)

● **How did it feel to be the team that fought to get into the chairs?** (I was confused by the way the other team acted; it wasn't as much fun since the other team didn't fight back.)

● **Which team won?** (I guess both did, since they were playing by different rules; our team won.)

● **In this game, the two teams played with different goals in mind. How is that like the difference between people who look out for only themselves, and those that try to honor and respect others?** (Sometimes it looks like the nice people are losing, but they're not; it confuses the selfish people because they can't figure out why others are being nice to them.)

● **In real life, which team are you usually most like? Explain.** (The nice team, I usually try to make everybody like me; the nice team, I'm not mean to anyone, even if they're mean to me.)

● **Do you think other people ever feel that you treat them like the rowdy team treated the other team? Explain.** (No, I'm not that bad; Maybe, I try to get my way a lot.)

Say: **The commandments we're looking at today go a lot deeper than just treating others nicely. We're going to**

ACTION AND REFLECTION
(10 to 15 minutes)

take a look at them now, and also see what Jesus had to say about them. As we do, I think we'll discover that the real "winning" team is the one that does things God's way.

ZOOBLADITE ZINGERS

Form three groups, pass out the "Zoobladite Zingers" handout (p. 33) and assign groups the following passages:

Group A—Exodus 20:12; Mark 7:8-13
Group B—Exodus 20:13; Matthew 5:21-22
Group C—Exodus 20:14; Matthew 5:27-28

If your class doesn't understand the term "commit adultery," explain it to them briefly. A good definition they'd understand is "having sex with someone you're not married to."

Say: **The Zoobladites still need your help! They understand this week's commandments pretty well, but they haven't studied what Jesus had to say about the commandments. Help them out by looking up your passages and filling in your answers to their questions.**

When groups have completed the handout, have them each report to the rest of the class. Then ask:

● **What principles do these commandments give us for maintaining good relationships with our parents? with other people?** (We need to obey our parents; stop hassling your parents; don't call people degrading names.)

Say: **We've seen the principles, now let's see how they apply to our lives.**

RESPECT AND HONOR ACROSTIC

Form groups of three or four. Give each group one sheet of paper and a pencil. Have half of the groups create an acrostic based on the word "respect." Each line should represent something teenagers can do to show more respect to other people. Have the other half of the groups create an acrostic based on the word "honor." Each line should represent something teenagers can do to honor others more.

Before kids begin their acrostics, read these definitions of respect and honor:

Respect—to show consideration for; avoid intruding upon or interfering with

Honor—to show high regard for; to treat with courtesy

When kids are finished, have group members each tell one way their other group members have shown them respect and honor. Then have group members each choose from their acrostic one way they'll work to show more respect and honor to their parents and others.

If you have time, have groups share their acrostics with the rest of the class.

☐ OPTION 1: PRAYER OF RESPECT

Close your session with prayer, having kids each briefly tell God aloud what they'll do or change in their life to show proper respect and honor for their parents and other people. After each individual's prayer, have the group pray, "Thanks, God, for (name)'s commitment to you."

☐ OPTION 2: PAIRS IN PRAYER

Pass out 3×5 cards and have kids each copy their acrostic to take with them. When they're ready, have kids form pairs with kids not in their previous group. Have kids each share which element of the acrostic they're especially going to work on in the coming week. Have kids each write a short prayer on the back of their partner's card. Then close with a moment of silent prayer as kids silently read the prayers their partners wrote.

C L O S I N G
(up to 5 minutes)

If You Still Have Time . . .

Playing Parent—Have your kids think about what it would be like to be one of their parents. Give them a few minutes to brainstorm ways they'd like to be treated by their children. Then form groups of two or three and let one person role play a teenager while one or two people role play a parent or parents trying to get more respect from the teenager.

Murder by Definition—Let your kids discuss what is murder and what isn't. Remind them of Jesus' comments in Matthew 5:21-22.

 **THE CHAIRS**

TEAM 1

This game is kind of like musical chairs, only we're going to play it in teams. Each round there'll be one chair less than we have people. The first team entirely eliminated loses. Do everything you can to help your team win. If there's an empty chair near you as you sit down, try to help your teammate get it instead of letting someone from the other team get it. If you end up without a chair, let everyone know how angry you are about it. Almost anything goes, but just don't pull a chair out from under anyone.

TEAM 2

This game is kind of like musical chairs, only we're going to play it in teams. Each round there'll be one chair less than we have people. The first team entirely eliminated wins. All the chairs must be filled when the music stops, so try to get the other team into the chairs before you have to sit down. Be courteous, even if the other team gets nasty. Remember, the object is to get your team eliminated first.

ZOOBLADITE ZINGERS

The Zoobladites are at it again! They're learning the Ten Commandments, but need help figuring out what else they need to know. See what you can do to answer their questions.

Commandment A: Honor your father and your mother (Exodus 20:12).
● What does Jesus say about this commandment (Mark 7:8-13)?
● How does what Jesus says about this commandment clarify how we look at it?
● How does a teenager who's obeying this commandment act toward his or her parents?

Commandment B: You shall not murder (Exodus 20:13).
● What does Jesus say about this commandment (Matthew 5:21-22)?
● How does what Jesus says about this commandment change the way we look at it?
● How does a teenager who's obeying what Jesus says about this commandment act toward other people?

Commandment C: You shall not commit adultery (Exodus 20:14).
● What does Jesus say about this commandment (Matthew 5:27-28)?
● How does what Jesus says about this commandment change the way we look at it?
● How does a teenager who's obeying what Jesus says about this commandment act toward people of the opposite sex?

LESSON 4

DON'T BE GREEDY

We live in a materialistic world. Better cars, better homes, nicer clothes, bigger boats, bigger bank accounts—nearly every public measure of success is based on things. But the last of the commandments tell us not to concentrate on what we have, or on what someone else has. God wants us to be content with what we have and to trust him for what we need. He wants us to treat others the way we'd want to be treated. And with God's help, junior highers can begin to do those things right now.

LESSON AIM

To help junior highers learn to trust God for the things they need, and to treat others the way they want to be treated.

OBJECTIVES

Students will:
- **discuss what it's like to have things stolen;**
- **experience stealing and having things stolen;**
- **explain today's commandments without using words; and**
- **write ways they can obey Exodus 20:15-17.**

BIBLE BASIS

EXODUS 20:15-17
MATTHEW 6:25-34
MATTHEW 7:12

Look up the following scriptures. Then read the background paragraphs to see how the passages relate to your junior highers and middle schoolers.

Exodus 20:15-17 lists the last of the Ten Commandments. Here God gives us important guidelines for living at peace with people around us. We're not to want or take what our neighbor has, but instead we're to be honest and upright, content with what God has given us.

Of all the commandments, none are more easy to apply to

teenagers than these. It's easy to want someone else's shoes, money or boyfriend. But kids can learn to center their lives on what God wants instead of what they want.

In **Matthew 6:25-34**, Jesus spells out why we can trust God to take care of us.

This beautiful passage illustrates for us why we don't need to worry about material things. It assures us God is in charge and that he cares for us. And when we put him first, God will make sure we have what we need.

Teenagers can get caught up in materialism, just like adults. This passage helps them put possessions in perspective.

In **Matthew 7:12**, Jesus describes what we know as the Golden Rule.

This verse, in Jesus' own words, sums up the Law and the Prophets. It certainly sums up today's commandments well.

If junior highers can learn to treat others the way they'd like to be treated, God will be pleased and relationships will be genuine.

THIS LESSON AT A GLANCE

Section	Minutes	What Students Will Do	Supplies
Opener (Option 1)	5 to 10	**Thief! Thief!**—Have their valuables taken away.	Paper sack
(Option 2)		**In The News**—Tear out and discuss reports of thefts from newspapers.	Newspapers
Action and Reflection	10 to 15	**Grab All You Can Get**—Steal candies from one another and discuss feelings.	Bag of M&M's candies
Bible Application	15 to 20	**Zoobladite Stew**—Explain today's commandments using skits or silent presentations.	Bibles
Commitment	5 to 10	**Thought Balloons**—Write on balloons specific ways to obey the commandments.	Balloons and markers
Closing (Option 1)	up to 5	**M&M's Revisited**—Feed each other candies.	Bag of M&M's candies
(Option 2)		**Sing a Song**—Sing songs celebrating God's commands.	Songbooks

The Lesson

☐ OPTION 1: THIEF! THIEF!

After kids have arrived, get out a paper sack and go around the room demanding that kids put their wallets and jewelry in the sack. Refuse to answer any questions, and appear to get angry when kids resist. Keep a straight face and be serious about your demands. Be sure no loose money is put in the sack—you need to be able to give everything back accurately later. But don't let kids think you're going to give it back.

When you've collected kids' valuables, wrap up the sack and make some comments like, "I've been needing a new car, and this will help," or "Now I've got enough to get that boat I've been wanting."

Set the bag aside as if you're really going to keep the things in it, and begin making small talk with the kids. Make it seem like you're trying to make kids forget you've just taken their things.

After a couple of minutes, ask:

● **How did it feel having me take your jewelry and wallets?** (Strange, I knew you were up to something; okay, I knew we'd get them back.)

● **How would it feel if you didn't ever get them back?** (I'd be mad; I'd really miss my watch.)

● **Have you ever taken something someone else had? Tell about it if you're willing.**

● **Have you ever wanted to take something someone else has?** (Lots of times; I never wanted what the rich kids have.)

As you return kids' things, say: **The commandments we're looking at today have to do with how we look at what other people have. And one of those commandments is about stealing.**

☐ OPTION 2: IN THE NEWS

Pass out the newspapers and have kids each tear out one article about people stealing things.

After a few minutes, have kids each read or summarize their article. Then discuss these questions:

● **Why do you think these people stole things?** (To get rich; to buy drugs.)

● **Do you think these people would like to have things stolen from them? Explain.** (No way; never.)

● **How would it feel to be the victim in one of these articles?** (Pretty bad; I'd want to get my stuff back.)

Say: **Today one of the commandments we're looking at is about stealing. And all of the commandments have to do with how we look at what other people have.**

GRAB ALL YOU CAN GET

Get out a big bag of M&M's candies or another attractive candy. Give kids each 10 pieces, and tell them that these candies represent all their riches. Let kids decide what each candy represents. For example, one candy might represent a home in Malibu; another, a yacht in Ft. Lauderdale; another, a diamond worth $800,000. Have kids each tell what at least one candy represents. Be sure to participate yourself.

Once all have named their riches, say: **You may not eat any of your own candy, and you may not hide it in any way. You cannot hold it in your hand, and it must always be visible to everyone else. But if you can manage to swipe someone else's candy, you can quickly gobble it down to keep him or her from getting it back. The object of the game is to get through the next three minutes with the highest total pieces of candy, either saved or eaten. You need to keep track of the number of candies you eat if you want to win.**

Give kids the go signal, and watch for the fireworks. Aggressively go after candy yourself.

When the three minutes are up, total the candies saved and eaten, and announce the winner. It's possible some kids will exaggerate the number of candies eaten. If kids complain about people cheating, talk about how this activity is like real life—where people cheat or feel cheated about what they earn. Then ask:

● **How did it feel when someone took one of your candies and ate it?** (I was mad; it was funny.)

● **How did it feel eating someone else's candy?** (It was great; it didn't bother me.)

● **How is this like the way people feel and act in real life?** (Lots of people just take what they want; people who steal don't think about others' feelings.)

● **How do you think God feels about this kind of behavior?** (He doesn't like it; angry because people are taking things that aren't theirs.)

Say: **Let's look in the Bible to see just how God does want us to act toward other people.**

ZOOBLADITE STEW

Say: **This time the Zoobladites have done it. They decided to ignore the Ten Commandments and take over the Earth. But they have a problem. There are only five of them and billions of us. To make it worse, their only weapon is a beam of energy that makes people laugh.**

You caught them when they were taking your stereo but they escaped with it. Even though your sides ache from laughing, you want to teach them a lesson. But you have another problem. They've been listening to too much loud music since they stole your stereo and they've all gone deaf. So we're going to try one more time to help

ACTION AND REFLECTION
(10 to 15 minutes)

BIBLE APPLICATION
(15 to 20 minutes)

them understand the right way to live.

Form three groups and assign one of these passages to each group: Exodus 20:15-17; Matthew 6:25-34; or Matthew 7:12. Have groups each put together a pantomime or a symbolic presentation to silently demonstrate the meaning of their passage to the Zoobladites. After every presentation, have the presenting group read aloud its passage.

Give groups about seven minutes to prepare, then have them give their skits or presentations. Then ask:

● **How do these things we've studied apply to your own lives?** (We need to be honest; we shouldn't steal or cheat; we should treat others the way we would like to be treated.)

Say: **Now we're going to look more specifically at how these apply to us.**

THOUGHT BALLOONS

Get out a balloon and a marker and have kids form a circle. If you have more than 10 kids, form circles of five to 10 kids and give each group a balloon and a marker.

Say: **I'm going to gently tap this balloon to someone and hand that person the marker. That person will write on the balloon one positive, specific way to strive to obey the teachings we've learned today. I'll start by writing one myself and numbering it with a "1." When the balloon comes to you, read aloud the last thing written on it, write something new and tap the balloon to someone else.**

Start by writing something such as "Be honest with everyone."

When all kids have written at least one thing, and are beginning to have trouble thinking of things, give them another balloon and say: **On this balloon, write something you honestly like about a person in the circle, then tap the balloon to that person. For example, you might write, "great laugh" or "faithful friend." No one can receive the balloon twice.**

When the balloon has gone around the circle, affirm kids for their participation and honesty. Hang the balloons in the room as reminders of what you studied today.

☐ OPTION 1: M&M'S REVISITED

Give each person 10 M&M's candies. Kids aren't allowed to eat their own candies; instead, have them feed their candies to other kids. No one can give the same person more than two M&M's candies. If you have more than 10 kids, you might want to limit the giving to one M&M's candy per person. Remind kids that they're doing for others what they like having others do for them.

Close your class with prayer, asking God to help your kids be generous with others and content with what they have.

COMMITMENT
(5 to 10 minutes)

CLOSING
(up to 5 minutes)

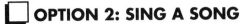

OPTION 2: SING A SONG

Wrap up your class by singing choruses related to the message of today's lesson, such as "Thy Word," "This Is My Commandment," and "Love Command" (The Group Songbook).

Close with prayer, letting kids offer prayers of commitment and thanks to God.

If You Still Have Time . . .

Sing a New Song—Have your kids create a song based on the Ten Commandments, using the tune to "The Twelve Days of Christmas." Call it "The Ten Great Commandments." It'll be a great way to help kids remember all the commandments.

Course Reflection—Form a circle. Ask students to reflect on the past four lessons. Have them take turns completing the following sentences:

- Something I learned in this course is . . .
- If I could tell my friends about this course, I'd say . . .
- Something I'll do differently because of this course is . . .

BONUS IDEAS

Bonus Scriptures—The lessons focus on a select few scripture passages, but if you'd like to incorporate more Bible readings into the lessons, here are some suggestions:

● Psalm 1:1-2 (The psalmist describes people who meditate on God's law.)

● Psalm 19:7-8 (The psalmist describes God's law as perfect.)

● Matthew 5:23-26 (Jesus explains the law of reconciliation.)

● Matthew 5:43-48 (Jesus tells his followers to love their enemies and pray for them.)

● Mark 7:1-15 (Jesus criticizes the Pharisees' reinterpretation of the Law.)

● Romans 8:1-11 (Paul describes how Jesus' sacrifice fulfilled the law for us.)

● 1 John 5:3 (The writer tells us God's commandments are not burdensome.)

Same Commandments, New Words—Have your kids "translate" the Ten Commandments into language God might use to speak to kids today. Be sure kids keep to the meaning of the text and don't make their "translation" too frivolous.

Ten Commandments Theology—Have your pastor visit your class to explain how your church believes the Ten Commandments apply today. Help kids decide on questions ahead of time and give them to the pastor.

And Jesus Said—Lead your kids in a study of what Jesus said about the commandments. Use a concordance to look up references to the commandments in the gospels, and guide kids in sorting out how Jesus looked at the Law as a whole and at each individual commandment.

And Then There Are Laws—Take your kids to visit a session of your state legislature. Spend a couple of hours listening to the presentations and arguments. If possible, arrange a visit with a Christian legislator and discuss how God's laws affect the way he or she votes on your state's laws. After you return, compare the two ways of receiving laws—through God directly and through a group of people.

Commandments by Memory—The Ten Commandments fill 16 verses in Exodus 20:2-17. If kids memorize just four verses per week, they'll have all of the commandments memorized in

MEETINGS AND MORE

four weeks. Give kids prizes as incentives for memorizing the commandments, or use creative methods in class to help with their memorization such as creating actions to go with them or playing games that require kids to recite them.

Table Talk—Use the "Table Talk" handout (p. 18) for a parents night with your class. You might want to meet shortly after concluding the course. For some fun games to start off the evening, check out *Have-A-Blast Games* (Group Books). Have parents work through the handout with their kids, and let families report on what they discovered.

Scripture Songfest—Have a time of celebration, singing songs related to God's commandments and other scriptures. You could make a contest of it by having kids race to track down the scripture reference each song is based on.

It's the Law—Have a police officer visit your class to talk about law enforcement. If the officer is a Christian, you can discuss with him or her how human law enforcement is different from God's law enforcement. If the officer isn't a Christian, don't put him or her on the spot, just plan to make the comparison after the officer leaves.

Foul Play—Have groups of kids each create a skit that spoofs soap operas by showing the characters deliberately breaking each of the Ten Commandments. Have kids use the "Foul Play" handout (p. 44) to help them plan their skits. After skits have been prepared and presented, discuss the questions at the bottom of the sheet.

PARTY PLEASER

Zoobladite Zoo—Have kids dress up as they imagine the Zoobladites might look. Play trivia games based on what you learned about the commandments, letting all the Zoobladites report on what your class taught them over the weeks of this course. Serve far-out food, using food coloring to make normal foods look like something from outer space.

RETREAT IDEA

Commandment Attitudes—Plan a retreat concentrating on the attitudes behind the commandments. Divide your time into 11 segments. Use one segment for each commandment and the last one to pull everything together.

Set up few rules for the retreat, but carefully explain the reasoning behind them and discuss the attitudes the rules are designed to promote.

Play lots of games involving everyone in the fun. After playing several games, discuss how rules helped the games and how the lack of rules could destroy the fun. Let kids make up new games with as few rules as possible. Discuss how more rules are often necessary to make a game more fun.

Have kids work together to make a "Ten Commandments" cake. By using a 9x13-inch pan and a 9-inch round pan cut in half, it's easy to create a cake that looks like a stone tablet. Have kids decorate the cake and eat it for an evening snack.

Use your wrap-up session to lead kids toward a commitment to develop the attitudes God wants us to have—attitudes that will naturally result in following his commandments.

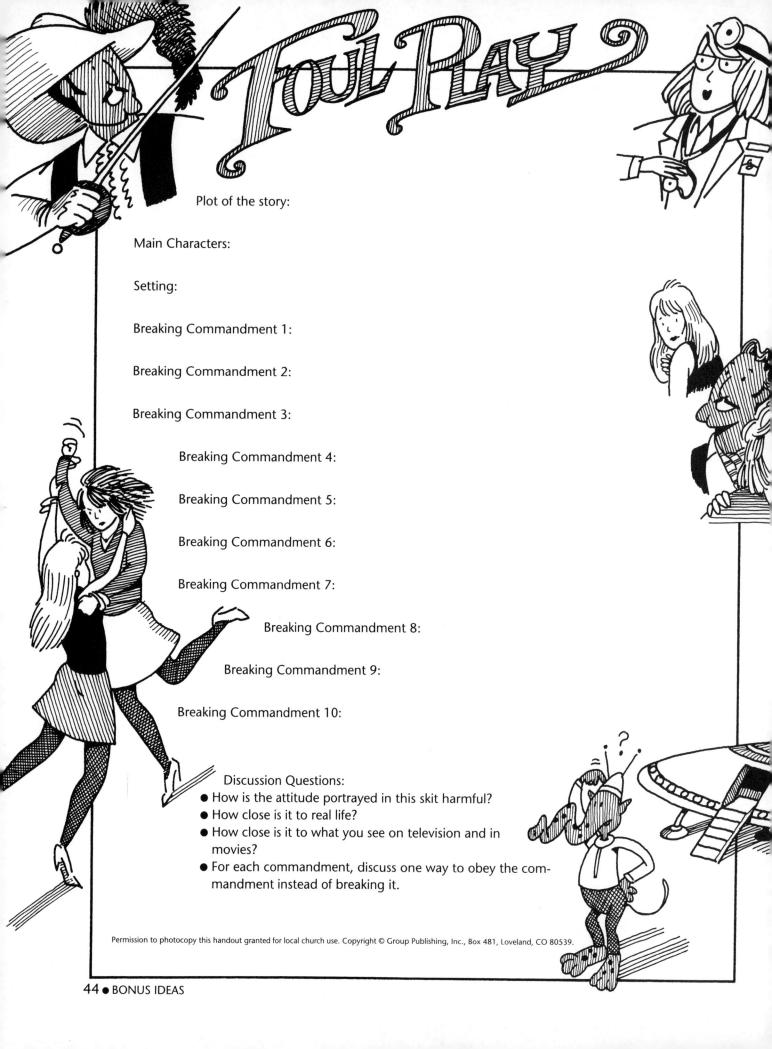

Foul Play

Plot of the story:

Main Characters:

Setting:

Breaking Commandment 1:

Breaking Commandment 2:

Breaking Commandment 3:

Breaking Commandment 4:

Breaking Commandment 5:

Breaking Commandment 6:

Breaking Commandment 7:

Breaking Commandment 8:

Breaking Commandment 9:

Breaking Commandment 10:

Discussion Questions:
- How is the attitude portrayed in this skit harmful?
- How close is it to real life?
- How close is it to what you see on television and in movies?
- For each commandment, discuss one way to obey the commandment instead of breaking it.

CURRICULUM REORDER—TOP PRIORITY

Order now to prepare for your upcoming Sunday school classes, youth ministry meetings, and weekend retreats! Each book includes all teacher and student materials—plus photocopiable handouts—for any size class!

FOR JUNIOR HIGH/MIDDLE SCHOOL:

Accepting Others: Beyond Barriers & Stereotypes
ISBN 1-55945-126-2

Advice to Young Christians: Exploring Paul's Letters
ISBN 1-55945-146-7

Applying the Bible to Life, ISBN 1-55945-116-5

Becoming Responsible, ISBN 1-55945-109-2

Bible Heroes: Joseph, Esther, Mary & Peter
ISBN 1-55945-137-8

Boosting Self-Esteem, ISBN 1-55945-100-9

Building Better Friendships, ISBN 1-55945-138-6

Can Christians Have Fun?, ISBN 1-55945-134-3

Caring for God's Creation, ISBN 1-55945-121-1

Christmas: A Fresh Look, ISBN 1-55945-124-6

Competition, ISBN 1-55945-133-5

Dealing With Death, ISBN 1-55945-112-2

Dealing With Disappointment, ISBN 1-55945-139-4

Doing Your Best, ISBN 1-55945-142-4

Drugs & Drinking, ISBN 1-55945-118-1

Evil and the Occult, ISBN 1-55945-102-5

Genesis: The Beginnings, ISBN 1-55945-111-4

Guys & Girls: Understanding Each Other
ISBN 1-55945-110-6

Handling Conflict, ISBN 1-55945-125-4

Heaven & Hell, ISBN 1-55945-131-9

Is God Unfair?, ISBN 1-55945-108-4

Love or Infatuation?, ISBN 1-55945-128-9

Making Parents Proud, ISBN 1-55945-107-6

Making the Most of School, ISBN 1-55945-113-0

Materialism, ISBN 1-55945-130-0

The Miracle of Easter, ISBN 1-55945-143-2

Miracles!, ISBN 1-55945-117-3

Peace & War, ISBN 1-55945-123-8

Peer Pressure, ISBN 1-55945-103-3

Prayer, ISBN 1-55945-104-1

Reaching Out to a Hurting World, ISBN 1-55945-140-8

Sermon on the Mount, ISBN 1-55945-129-7

Suicide: The Silent Epidemic, ISBN 1-55945-145-9

Telling Your Friends About Christ, ISBN 1-55945-114-9

The Ten Commandments, ISBN 1-55945-127-0

Today's Faith Heroes, ISBN 1-55945-141-6

Today's Media: Choosing Wisely, ISBN 1-55945-144-0

Today's Music: Good or Bad?, ISBN 1-55945-101-7

What Is God's Purpose for Me?, ISBN 1-55945-132-7

What's a Christian?, ISBN 1-55945-105-X

FOR SENIOR HIGH:

1 & 2 Corinthians: Christian Discipleship
ISBN 1-55945-230-7

Angels, Demons, Miracles & Prayer, ISBN 1-55945-235-8

Changing the World, ISBN 1-55945-236-6

Christians in a Non-Christian World
ISBN 1-55945-224-2

Christlike Leadership, ISBN 1-55945-231-5

Communicating With Friends, ISBN 1-55945-228-5

Counterfeit Religions, ISBN 1-55945-207-2

Dating Decisions, ISBN 1-55945-215-3

Dealing With Life's Pressures, ISBN 1-55945-232-3

Deciphering Jesus' Parables, ISBN 1-55945-237-4

Exodus: Following God, ISBN 1-55945-226-9

Exploring Ethical Issues, ISBN 1-55945-225-0

Faith for Tough Times, ISBN 1-55945-216-1

Forgiveness, ISBN 1-55945-223-4

Getting Along With Parents, ISBN 1-55945-202-1

Getting Along With Your Family, ISBN 1-55945-233-1

The Gospel of John: Jesus' Teachings
ISBN 1-55945-208-0

Hazardous to Your Health: AIDS, Steroids & Eating Disorders, ISBN 1-55945-200-5

Is Marriage in Your Future?, ISBN 1-55945-203-X

Jesus' Death & Resurrection, ISBN 1-55945-211-0

The Joy of Serving, ISBN 1-55945-210-2

Knowing God's Will, ISBN 1-55945-205-6

Life After High School, ISBN 1-55945-220-X

Making Good Decisions, ISBN 1-55945-209-9

Money: A Christian Perspective, ISBN 1-55945-212-9

Movies, Music, TV & Me, ISBN 1-55945-213-7

Overcoming Insecurities, ISBN 1-55945-221-8

Psalms, ISBN 1-55945-234-X

Real People, Real Faith, ISBN 1-55945-238-2

Responding to Injustice, ISBN 1-55945-214-5

Revelation, ISBN 1-55945-229-3

School Struggles, ISBN 1-55945-201-3

Sex: A Christian Perspective, ISBN 1-55945-206-4

Today's Lessons From Yesterday's Prophets
ISBN 1-55945-227-7

Turning Depression Upside Down, ISBN 1-55945-135-1

What Is the Church?, ISBN 1-55945-222-6

Who Is God?, ISBN 1-55945-218-8

Who Is Jesus?, ISBN 1-55945-219-6

Who Is the Holy Spirit?, ISBN 1-55945-217-X

Your Life as a Disciple, ISBN 1-55945-204-8

Order today from your local Christian bookstore, or write: Group Publishing, Box 485, Loveland, CO 80539.

Blast away boredom with these upcoming scripture-based topics:

For Senior High:

- Exodus: Following God
- Acts: The Early Church
- Loving Life

- Living in a Non-Christian World
- Communicating With Friends
- What Revelation Reveals

For Junior High/Middle School:

- Materialism
- Heaven & Hell
- Competition and Sports

- Sex, Love and Infatuation
- Finding a Sense of Purpose
- Can Christians Have Fun?

For more details write:

Box 485 ● Loveland, CO 80539 ● 800-747-6060, ext. 427

PUT FAITH INTO ACTION...

...with Group's **Projects With a Purpose™ for Youth Ministry**.

Want to try something different with your 7th—12th grade classes? Group's NEW **Projects With a Purpose™ for Youth Ministry** offers four-week courses that really get kids into their faith. Each **Project With a Purpose** course gives you tools to facilitate a project that will provide a direct, purposeful learning experience. Teenagers will discover something significant about their faith while learning the importance of working together, sharing one another's troubles, and supporting one another in love...plus they'll have lots of fun!

Use for Sunday school classes, midweek meetings, home Bible studies, youth groups, retreats, or any time you want to help teenagers discover more about their faith. Your kids will learn more about each other. They'll practice the life skill of working together. And you'll be rewarded with the knowledge that you're providing a life-changing, faith-building experience for your church's teenagers.

Acting Out Jesus' Parables
Strengthen your teenagers' faith as they are challenged to understand the parables' descriptions of the Christian life. Explore such key issues as the value of humility, the importance of hope, and the relative unimportance of wealth.   ISBN 1-55945-147-5

Celebrating Christ With Youth-Led Worship
Kids love to celebrate. Birthdays. Dating. A new car. For Christians, Jesus is the ultimate reason to celebrate. And as kids celebrate Jesus, they'll grow closer to him—an excitement that will be shared with the whole congregation.   ISBN 1-55945-410-5

Checking Your Church's Pulse
Your teenagers will find new meaning for their faith and build greater appreciation for their church with this course. Interviews with congregational members will help your teenagers, and your church, grow together.   ISBN 1-55945-408-3

Serving Your Neighbors
Strengthen the "service heart" in your teenagers and watch as they discover the joy and value of serving. Your teenagers will appreciate the importance of serving others as they follow Jesus' example.   ISBN 1-55945-406-7

Sharing Your Faith Without Fear
Teenagers don't have to be great orators to share with others what God's love means to them. And teenagers can express their faith through everyday actions and lifestyles without fear of rejection.   ISBN 1-55945-409-1

Teaching Teenagers to Pray
Watch as your teenagers develop strong, effective prayer lives as you introduce them to the basics of prayer. As teenagers explore the depth and excitement of real prayer, they'll learn how to pray with and for others.   ISBN 1-55945-407-5

Teenagers Teaching Children
Teach your teenagers how to share the Gospel with children. Through this course, your teenagers will learn more about their faith by teaching others, and they'll learn lessons about responsibility and develop teaching skills to last a lifetime.   ISBN 1-55945-405-9

Videotaping Your Church Members' Faith Stories
Teenagers will enjoy learning about their congregation—and become players in their church's faith story with this exciting video project. And, they'll learn the depth and power of God's faithfulness to his people.   ISBN 1-55945-239-0

Order today from your local Christian bookstore, or write: Group Publishing, Box 485, Loveland, CO 80539.